Boss Moms Club

Boss Moms Club

A Parenting Guide for Working Moms

KRISTINA BUCKNER

Library of Congress Cataloging *status pending*
Credits: Author Kristina Buckner, Editor Cecilia Buckner, Photographer Rich Soublet, Photographer Kristina Buckner, Photographer Mariah Tims
Boss Moms Club

A Parenting Guide for Working Moms
ISBN
979-8-218-42891-4 paperback
979-8-218-42866-2 ebook
979-8-218-42894-5 audiobook

Boss Moms Club Podcast

This book is dedicated to my son Eric.
From a child raising a child, I did my very best at raising you and I know I wasn't perfect. Thank you for your patience as I figured the whole mom thing out. We grew up together. You have made me so proud of the man you are today. I hope I have made you proud too. I love you so much.

Kristina, 17 celebrating Eric's 2nd bday

"Everything That Lives Grows"
-KRISTINA BUCKNER

CONTENTS

PREFACE

Let me first say thank you for allowing me to enter your space. You picked up my book or clicked on the download button. Thank you. One thing 2020 taught me was to not take my time for granted and to use my time wisely! Throughout my life, I admit to making many mistakes. To your benefit, I will tell you my secrets to help prevent you from doing the same.

Once a teen mom, now a mother of two; an attorney and an 11-year-old aspiring doctor and entrepreneur, I have a vast amount of experience in motherhood. Being a young mother at 15 years old was difficult for me and my son was the motivation in my life. Despite my youth, I was determined not to be a statistic. I was resolved to make it on my own and to keep my family together.

Having been raised in a single-parent home myself, I often questioned how I was able to break this cycle. Truth be told, I didn't. There were many years when I believed that the home I built with my partner was breaking the family curse, only to later find out I was wrong and found myself back in the shoes of my mother. It appears that even with the success of my first child, I would still be destined to raise my kids alone. I plan to delve deeper into this topic in my next book.

INTRODUCTION

In my series of guides and books, you will learn how I manage to find balance in motherhood and my hope is that it helps you do the same. Want to know my secret? I never balance.

On this journey, we will explore the art of balancing life, work, and momhood. I understand the complexities you face daily, the demands on your time and energy, and the constant tug-of-war between your various roles. Fear not, because you are not alone. Countless moms around the world are navigating the same path, seeking harmony amidst the chaos, and striving to create a fulfilling life for themselves and their families. Stop caring about what society wants you to be and start living your life unapologetically.

Are you a mom juggling countless responsibilities and feeling overwhelmed by the pressures of motherhood? Look no further than "Boss Moms Club" for the ultimate guide to relieving the fears of motherhood and reclaiming your sense of empowerment. I was once a teen mom and am now a mother of two; an attorney and an aspiring doctor and entrepreneur. I understand the struggle to stay focused on your goals while being both superwoman and a mom. **Let me help you save the child, the day and you.**

In this transformative guide, I provide a roadmap for busy moms to find balance and joy in their lives. Through a blend of personal anecdotes, practical advice, and empowering insights, you'll discover how to embrace the challenges of motherhood while still nurturing your own dreams and desires.

Being a Boss Mom means embracing both your strengths and your softness, recognizing that these qualities are not mutually exclusive. By bringing empathy, effective communication, and a nurturing spirit to your role as a mom, you create a supportive and empowering environment where everyone can thrive.

More than just a how-to guide, "Boss Moms Club" is a manifesto for empowerment. It's a reminder that you can be a devoted mom and a fierce woman simultaneously. So, join the club and rediscover the freedom and fulfillment that comes with balancing all facets of life like a true boss mom. **I have held many titles throughout my career, but there is only one title I am most proud of - Mom.**

Join me on this journey of mom-hood. Let's be friends.

Chapter One

THE POWER OF NOW

Being in quarantine was the change that a lot of us needed. What used to be a wait and see, quickly turned into a plan. And as crazy as this sounds, I am thankful for it. I am not thankful for the illness that struck many and that still affects many lives today. I am thankful for the clear mind that I obtained during one of the most uncertain times in history. The COVID 19 Pandemic.

There is nothing more powerful than being your own boss and my time spent during quarantine helped me realize that. The journey may not always be smooth, and there will be obstacles to overcome, but with the power of now, you have the opportunity to transform your life and create a future filled with joy and personal fulfillment.

I believe that by investing in yourself, you are also investing in your children's future. You are doing so by demonstrating the importance of self-worth and showing them that dreams are worth pursuing. You deserve to explore various aspects of self-investment, from nurturing your physical and mental well-being to pursuing your passions and personal growth.

Find the power in now - the power to make positive changes, the power to pursue your dreams, and the power to create a life that aligns with your values and aspirations. It's not about waiting for the perfect moment or for your children to grow older. The time is now, because today is all you have.

By investing in yourself, you create a ripple effect of positivity that extends beyond your own life and touches the lives of those around you. I challenge you to step outside your comfort zone, rediscover your passions, and embrace the unique qualities that make you who you are. Together, we'll create a roadmap for self-investment that allows you to find fulfillment and purpose while nurturing your role as a mother.

Motherhood is a beautiful transformative journey. From the moment you hold your child in your arms, your life changes in ways you never imagined. Your days become a whirlwind of diapers, feedings, school runs, and endless to-do lists. In the midst of this beautiful chaos, it's easy to lose sight of yourself and put your own needs on hold and sometimes that hold is permanent. But here's the truth: You are important, and your dreams and aspirations matter. You can create a life that nourishes your soul, fuels your passions, and allows you to be the best version of yourself for both you and your family.

My purpose is to share strategies for carving out time for yourself amidst the demands of motherhood, that will help you navigate the guilt and self-doubt that often accompany prioritizing your own needs. Throughout this journey, we'll explore practical tips, inspiring stories, and expert advice to guide you along the way. We are setting a powerful example for our children and creating a legacy of self-love and resilience. Your dreams matter, and it's time to make them a priority. The power to transform your life is within you, and it starts right now.

The Power of Now

Chapter Two

IS THAT SPILLED MILK?

Quarantine Troubles

Well don't cry over it.... There was a time when I needed to do everything right and if I didn't, it was the end of the world. What really changed this way of thinking for me was my days spent in quarantine. If you were like me, single and taking care of a child under 10 years old, you might agree with me when I say, life added 10 more pounds and I mean that literally too! To avoid the feeling of complete panic I found myself cooking Thanksgiving dinners in the Spring and logging into Zoom happy hours and concerts in the afternoon with my favorite music artists from the 90's. Like many of us, I was still somehow able to smile and laugh. I attributed this to my ability to focus on what mattered most, my family. I needed to keep a clear head. I turned off the TV.

I didn't know what I was going to do. I was already the head of my household and now added the roles of full-time teacher, full-day chef and maid. I would also like to add that I never received the salary increases for all of the added responsibilities, who should I report that to? Well, I would respond by saying me, myself and I. Now don't get me wrong, I'm not complaining. I simply raise this question because moms have evolved from stay at home moms to now working moms. And although society acknowledges this shift, many moms still don't catch a break.

Moms possess the strength of a lion. We are fearless, compassionate beings who take on the world's challenges and find a way even when we have our backs against the wall. But it is only AFTER we make our mistakes that we become stronger. We overcome our challenges and we continue to play the cards that we've been dealt.

Kind of like the game of spades. I would say that I am a good spades player, but I must admit that I play a better game with a good spades partner. WE win more games together. Now I'm not running to the next nearby casino anytime soon, but what I'm trying to say is that moms are strong, but we're even stronger with a good partner. So if we find ourselves doing this mom thing alone, just know that we're going to figure it out, because moms are resilient.

As a part of being resilient, I needed to show my daughter that when I opened the front door, it was a little crazy outside, but at home we were safe. We learned to garden and grow fresh herbs together. And instead of keeping our eyes locked to the virus updates that consumed the television screen, we made vision boards. Our boards included our goals for the coming years and where we wanted to travel, like Hawaii. We took out old magazines and markers from the dusty crafting bins in the garage and discovered that there was more to life than what was going on outside. Life was more about what we were doing in the moment. We were finding ourselves.

It was only after this experience that I truly learned what my role as a working mother and entrepreneur really looked like. Schools were shut down and business offices were closed. The panic of WTF am I going to do hit me fast!

The worry of what's going to happen if I get sick kicked in quickly. Or even quicker, was the thought of my daughter getting sick, who was considered high risk. Her little immune system has always been on the sensitive side since the day she was born. I couldn't think of her getting sick, especially not at a time like this. What was I going to do?? Well, just like most of you - I took things day by day. Before the pandemic, I was spending many hours away from home and spending less hours with my "why" - my daughter.

It was during quarantine that I realized that I am not perfect, and I am doing my best. I realized maybe there is a way I can spend more time with my daughter while not only making a living, but making a life. Maybe I don't have to be perfect, maybe?

Time is All We Have

Early morning trips at 6 am to Mariah's school to drop her off at the AM-PM program and then pick her up in the early evening were no more. And guess what, I was okay with that. The more time I spent with my daughter, I realized I hadn't known my daughter at all. I mean I knew her, but I didn't know her. Does that make sense? It didn't take long before the bells went off in my head and I began brainstorming on how I would survive if this situation got worse. How could I manage to be the mom I want to be vs. the mom I had to be?

One morning as I sat down enjoying breakfast with Mariah, I paused. Have you ever had a moment where you were listening to someone talk, but you were so much into the moment that you got caught up in another world?

Yes? Okay, so yeah, that happened. As Mariah was talking to me, all I could think about was how many more moments like this I wanted at the kitchen table with her without the feeling of being rushed. Before the day of stress would naturally pull me away from her - it hadn't this time. The mystery person who usually grabs me away from my daughter, so I can rush to get to the office didn't show up. I thought this mystery person would be late, but for months, the person didn't show up at all. It was just me and Mariah. And I loved that.

Not until now, did I truly learn the meaning of the saying, don't cry over spilled milk. With so much going on in the world and with the uncertainty of my plain existence during quarantine, I realized something. It's much easier to wipe up the mess and move on than to continue holding on to the day's mishaps. This only leads to a continued pour of what you don't want, a mess!

Being a working mom comes with its challenges. Be a boss and run the day. Don't let the day run you.

Chapter Three

BALANCE

Congratulations! As a mom, you play one of the most important roles in the world.

You juggle countless responsibilities, from raising your children to managing a career and maintaining a household. It's no secret that being a mother can be both immensely rewarding and incredibly challenging. In the midst of it all, finding balance becomes an essential pursuit.

Balancing these vital aspects of your life is not about achieving perfection or having it all figured out. Mom-hood is about learning not to cry over spilled milk, so you can enjoy the fruits of life…The milk may have spilled, but wipe it up before it gets sour. It's about finding what works best for you and your unique circumstances, and discovering strategies that empower you to thrive as a mother, a professional, and an individual.

Honolulu, Hawaii -Kristina and Mariah
during quarantine - COVID 19, year 2020.

It's about embracing the inevitable ups and downs, and learning to adapt, grow, and enjoy the journey. And just as if you were preparing for a nice hike in warm or cold weather, be prepared for a forecast of rain.

Procrastination is the enemy. Through years of navigating motherhood, I've gained many valuable skills, but one stands out: recognizing when procrastination has started to distort my reality. Whether it's making excuses for unfinished tasks, sidelining my goals, or leaving a basket of clean clothes waiting to be folded on the edge of the bed, the signs are all too clear. Though I haven't yet fully mastered this challenge, acknowledging its presence is the first step in winning the battle. I won't let it defeat me, and neither should you.

After raising my oldest child, I was able to tweak a few templates for my youngest. Now of course, I am not perfect by any means. Even now I make my mistakes as a parent, but what I do now is very different from what I did years ago. The milk is going to spill so why not be prepared? I am not saying that you will be able to avoid every spill, but if you are prepared - we can save that milk for the cookies later on.

Survival Kit

1. **Shared digital calendar.** For my 10-year old I created an email account for her and we share calendars. She has all of her activities from gymnastics to school tests blocked off on her calendar with her own reminders. I attached her calendar to mine, so I see it everyday. I even invite her to her own doctor appointments and play dates.

2. **A weekly meal calendar.** We have our meals planned 7 days in advance. This truly helps with after-school activities and events that are on the agenda. What's offered at school? What days are homemade? My kiddo is a pescatarian, so this is a must.

3. **Include your child in your work activities.** From filling envelopes, organizing and creating to-do lists, my daughter helps me run my business. By doing this, she learns the process and we spend time together.

4. **Time blocking.** What's not on the calendar does not exist.

5. **Me time.** Is there such a thing? If you're anything like me, getting out of the house for a night out is rare. I have realized that time away from being a mom is a necessity. Society has separated the woman from the mom and that has left moms displaced in their emotions without anywhere to go. We were women before we became selfless moms who sacrificed everything for these little humans we gave life to. Dress up and get outside. Not only do you need it, you deserve it!

6. **Plan your clothes for the week.** Remember when you laid out your clothes and shoes with excitement for the first day of school? How much smoother would your mornings be if everyone in your home did this everyday of the week? Mornings are already hectic. Keep the morning simple, so you can enjoy one another, because sooner or later you will be separated by that mystery person who takes you away from your family... the J.O.B.

7. **Balance.** Guess what? There is no such thing as balance. Instead, I choose to move with the flow of life and adjust. Overall, we never balance. And I'm okay with that.

Chapter Four

MONEY SAVING TIPS

Overall, saving money provides mothers with a sense of control, stability and the ability to plan for our future. It empowers us to make informed financial decisions and create a more secure and fulfilling life for ourselves and our families.

Wanna Be Saved?

1. **Create a Budget.** Establish a monthly budget to track your income and expenses. This will help you identify areas where you can cut back and save money.

2. **Meal Planning and Cooking at Home.** Plan your meals in advance and cook at home as much as possible. This is often cheaper than eating out or ordering takeout. Look for budget-friendly recipes and consider batch cooking to save time and money.

3. **Buy in Bulk.** Purchase non-perishable items, such as pantry staples, toiletries, and cleaning supplies, in bulk. This can help you save money in the long run, as bulk purchases often come at a discounted price.

4. **Explore Free or Low-Cost Activities.** Look for free or low-cost activities in your community, such as local parks, libraries, and community centers. These venues often offer programs and events for children at little to no cost.

5. **Set Savings Goals.** Establish specific savings goals for yourself, whether it's for emergencies, future expenses, or long-term financial plans. Having a clear objective can help you stay motivated and help you make smarter spending decisions. Remember, saving money is a gradual process, and small changes can add up over time. It's important to find a balance between saving and maintaining a reasonable quality of life for you and your family.

6. **Separate the dough.** Create a separate account for free spending. Use this account for eating out, shopping and entertainment. This amount will be allocated in your budget. When this account runs short, don't dip!

Look up in the sky, it's a bird, it's a plane.

Let's face it, being a mom can be expensive and if you're not setting money aside every month towards your own personal well-being, you may find yourself stuck in a never ending cycle of feeling depleted. We don't want to lose you to the streets of the hood - tighten up.

Allocating a budget for your personal well-being is equally crucial as the funds devoted to your children's lunch expenses. Neglecting self-care can lead to costly consequences. Just as it's vital to prevent a car's tires from going flat, ensuring your vitality remains intact is essential. Maintain a consistent self-care routine throughout the month to keep yourself on track and avoid becoming overwhelmed by life's demands.

Don't come to the hood unprepared.

Chapter Five

SELF-CARE TIPS

This can often be confused as just a physical act of a massage, but don't be mistaken. How you treat your soul and your mind should also take great care. The seven self-care practices for every area of your life involve social, physical, mental, spiritual, emotional, home environment and financial self-care. Learn to take care of yourself the right way. Self-care is not a luxury... it is a must!

I discovered that just as easy as it is for us to write down the grocery list or the things we need to do around the house, we can write down all the ways we can take care of ourselves. So get those wish list items onto your chore list. Break your chores up if you have to, but do them.

Taking care of yourself should be a routine task just like the oil changes on your car. Well maybe not that analogy as I've never been the best at that.

Mind Chores

- **See a Therapist.** No, you're not crazy. Having someone you can talk to and have an unbiased opinion or ears to listen to may be the release that you need.

- **Read a book.** I prefer self-help books, but rather your readings be fiction or not, you may find enjoyment in what someone else has to say.

- **Open the blinds.** Sun just feels so good doesn't it? Stop sitting in the dark and open up the blinds.

- **Eat at a new restaurant.** I love food so this to me is a no-brainer. The ambiance and service of being waited on makes me feel special. We wait on our kiddos all the time. Go treat yourself.

- **Give someone a hug.** This feeling gives a sense of comfort

- **Write daily gratitudes.** What are you thankful for? It's easy to give the most attention to the things we don't have, but being thankful for what you do have naturally brings good vibes. Try writing a personal note to someone you know and tell them how grateful you are for them.

- **Meditation.** Find a quiet space and release the noise from the inside.

- **Motivational podcast.** Better productivity and a focused day can be motivated by a great podcast. Oftentimes, this is where new habits and ideas are birthed.

- **No TV in the bedroom.** Just as we use our remotes to turn off the TV, we need to turn off our minds. A TV in the place you rest makes it harder to turn off, literally.

- **Purge items and donate.** Out with the old and in with the new. Giving to those who are in need, while clearing our spaces for something new, releases stress. Spring cleaning can be done anytime of the year.

- **Daily affirmations.** Positive thinking is sometimes necessary to remind us of the things we already know, but have forgotten. You are strong, you are beautiful - say it daily!

- **Plants for your spaces.** There's something to be said about a beautiful plant or flower. Plants are natural air purifiers and they reduce stress. They remind us that we are living and everything that is living grows.

- **Order dinner in.** Take a break.

- **Declutter.** Even I get stuck with a pile of laundry to fold. Being reminded of this task can get cumbersome. Clean it up so you can start fresh and focus on what truly matters and needs your time.

- **Say "No".** If you don't say no, you will become the people pleaser and while there is nothing wrong with that, you will be left with nothing for yourself. Stop doing that. Say "No" sometimes.

- **Watch a good movie.** Sometimes we need to remove ourselves from the reality of the world and our circumstances. Even better - if you can do this with some friends.

- **Buy yourself flowers.** Flowers naturally brighten upon the room. So brighten up your mood and give yourself some flowers. I do this every week.

Body Chores

- **Massage.** By a professional or your partner - massages have proven to bring many benefits to our physical and mental well-being.

- **Hair care.** Tired of the same mom ponytail? Go to the salon!

- **Healthy eating.** How you feel starts with what you eat.

- **Medical care.** How can you feel your best if you still haven't had the annual physical or pap smear?

- **Stop hitting snooze.** Every hit on the snooze button is a lost opportunity.

- **A walk alone.** Clear your mind and have a moment to yourself. You could even go on a nice run.

- **Try yoga.** Stretching helps protect us from injuries .

- **Exercise.** This promotes physical and emotional well-being. Easier said than done, start small then work your way up to a routine.

- **Tea with honey.** Not only does it taste good, but studies show, depending on the tea of your choice, it can have many benefits.

- **Sit in silence.** Silence encourages calmness, supports health, and boosts creativity.

- **Get a puppy.** I am not responsible for the responsibilities that come with pet ownership, but having an animal that always greets you with a wagging tail when you're down is always a good idea.

- **Dance.** Don't know how? Take a class.

- **Skin care routine.** Does your teen have a better skin care routine than you?

- **Vitamin D.** As a control for emotions, lack of vitamin D is linked to depression, fatigue and hairlessness. Be sure to get your levels checked and correct them when prompted by your physician. Iron too.

Soul Chores

- **Spiritual connection.** Feeling connected may be your solution to loneliness.

- **Travel.** Make a list of places you want to travel and go. Go with your partner or grab your kids and make it a family trip.

- **Say "hi" to a stranger.** Why not? And if you're feeling really nice, try smiling while you're doing it.

- **Cook a new meal.** I don't know what it is, but cooking brings me peace. Creativity can spiral to great lengths after you've prepared an amazing meal. It can be yummy too. For an added bonus, include your kids for a fun night of mom chef. No kids around? I heard chef gone wild is fun too.

- **DIY project.** Find something that YOU enjoy doing and if you already have a hobby to enjoy, but haven't had time to get to it, do that.

- **Join Boss Moms Club.** Become a part of a community where you can feed your mind, body and soul.

Chapter Six

SEX IN THE HOOD...
MOTHERHOOD

I remember being a kid, sneaking my way into adult conversations trying to hear what it was all about and hearing the noises coming from my mother's bedroom. What was going on in there anyway? As I got older, I found out on my own and pretty early too. I was a mom before I finished high school. This once was embarrassing to mention. Now, it's liberating.

So what about sex?

It is important for mothers to feel deserving of their physical needs, including sex and intimacy, especially after having children because these aspects are fundamental to human nature and our overall well-being. Society leaves us to believe that mothers stay home with the children and that self enjoyment of sex and intimacy comes last or not at all. Single moms get it the worst in my opinion. Where are her kids?" And "what are you doing out? Always seem to be the questions asked by the onlookers, but tell me something - How does a single mother un-single herself? She un-singles herself by getting out of the house, that's how! If the bar isn't your thing, go on a brunch date with friends and be open to meeting someone new. Yes, I kind of made up that word un-single, but you get the point.

It is important for us humans to engage in physical intimacy and experience romantic connections that can bring joy, happiness, and a sense of fulfillment. Mothers are no exception to this! Recognizing and honoring our own needs helps us maintain a strong sense of self and enhances our overall well-being.

Physical affection, intimacy, and feeling loved are vital. Engaging in these aspects of life allows mothers to feel valued, desired, and supported. I like to feel desired, don't you? Improved self-esteem, reduced stress, and a positive outlook are all products of a life that includes social and intimate relationships. So go ahead and get that freak him dress out of the closet and rock it out tonight with your friend… or for your man.

When women feel loved and emotionally supported, we are more present and engaged as parents. Meeting our own physical and emotional needs enables us to approach parenting with a positive mindset, increased energy (especially if we are sexually charged) and a stronger emotional connection with our children.

It is crucial to recognize that every individual's experiences and choices may vary. Some mothers may prioritize their physical needs and choose to engage in dating and intimacy, while others may not feel ready or desire such experiences. And that's okay!

As a mother, finding time for intimacy with your partner can feel like an impossible task. Juggling childcare, household chores, and possibly even work responsibilities can leave you feeling exhausted and stretched thin. However, maintaining a strong connection with your partner is crucial for both your relationship and your own well-being.

How to Survive the Hood...Sex in the Hood

1. **Schedule Intimate Time.** Just as you schedule other important appointments and commitments, prioritize intimate time with your partner by adding it to your calendar. Whether it's a weekly date night or a quiet evening at home after the kids are asleep, setting aside dedicated time for each other helps ensure that intimacy doesn't get lost in the chaos of daily life.

2. **Get Creative.** Intimacy doesn't always have to mean a lengthy romantic evening. Look for opportunities to connect with your partner in small, meaningful ways throughout the day. Whether it's a quick hug or midday quickie. A loving text message, flirty message or a spontaneous kiss will also go a long way. These moments of connection can help keep the spark alive even when time is limited.

3. **Delegate and Prioritize.** Don't be afraid to ask for help when you need it. Enlist the support of family members, friends, or babysitters to take care of the kids for a few hours so you can have some quality time with your partner. Remember that it's okay to prioritize your relationship and your own needs occasionally.

4. **Communicate Openly.** Talk to your partner about your desire for intimacy and your concerns about finding the time. Open

communication is essential for understanding each other's needs and finding creative solutions together. Your partner may have insights or ideas that you hadn't considered, so approach the conversation with an open mind.

5. **Let Go of Guilt.** It's common for mothers to feel guilty about taking time for themselves or their relationships, but it's important to remember that self-care and intimacy are vital for your overall happiness and well-being. Let go of the guilt and allow yourself to enjoy the moments you share with your partner without reservation. Before you were a mom you were a woman. Swap out of your mom pants for a moment and find out who YOU are again.

Casual Sexual Relationships.

When it comes to casual sexual relationships, it's essential to consider your own values, boundaries, and emotional well-being. Here are some things to keep in mind:

1. **Know Your Boundaries.** Before engaging in any sexual activity, be clear about your own boundaries and what you're comfortable with. Communicate your expectations and desires openly with your partner to ensure that both parties are on the same page.

2. **Practice Safe Sex.** Protect your health and well-being. Use condoms and other forms of contraception consistently to reduce the risk of sexually transmitted infections and unintended pregnancy.

3. **Consider Emotional Consequences.** While casual sexual relationships can be enjoyable and fulfilling for some people, they may not be right for everyone. Consider how you might feel emotionally after engaging in casual sex and whether you're prepared

to handle any potential consequences. Nothing is worse than getting attached to a man who is emotionally unavailable. Have the conversation before jumping all in.

4. **Be Mindful of Your Child's Well-Being.** As a parent, your child's well-being is your top priority. Consider how your dating life and any casual sexual relationships may impact your child and take steps to ensure that their needs are always prioritized.

Ultimately, the decision to engage in casual sexual relationships is a personal one, and there's no, one-size-fits-all answer (well maybe there is, just kidding). Trust your instincts, prioritize your own well-being and that of your child, and make choices that align with your values and goals.

Romance & Marriage. *Sex In The Hood* is about respecting and supporting each mother's unique journey as a key in fostering an environment where everyone feels empowered to make choices that align with their personal well-being and values. Don't wait for society's approval of your nights out, your dates with your husband, your new boo, or your quiet moments alone in your room. Seize control of your life and your youth at any age, without regrets.

After nearly two decades in a partnership with my ex, adjusting to the "new age" of dating has been a challenge. I yearn for romance, a stable family dynamic, and commitment, not just for myself but also for my daughter. I don't wish to navigate this journey solo as a single mom, yet, as I will delve into later, these are the cards I've been dealt. At times, I also feel myself lost in the hood until I remember - I know how to play spades.

Feeling loved and being touched is a need that's human in nature and **before you were a mom you were a woman** that was being touched and I would take a good guess to say that you were enjoying it too. If you've lost yourself in the hood, remember that it's never too late to find yourself again. Heels on - Glasses up - You deserve it!

Letter To My Whoadies

Dear Moms,

From self-care rituals that nourish the soul to savvy money-saving tips that stretch your budget further, Boss Moms Club covers every aspect of modern motherhood. As we dive into taboo topics like sex, reminding moms that they are not just caregivers, but vibrant women with needs and desires of their own, we have moments of self discovery. But it doesn't stop there. Boss Moms Club hosts events and wellness retreats that should be included on your chores list. If you would like us near you, go to www.bossmomsclub.com and add yourself to the mailing list for our future newsletters.

As a woman and a boss mom, I am not masculine. I am feminine and I can be passive. I can also be led by someone wearing the right shoes. A boss mom is simply a woman who is ambitious and gets the job done. By playing with the cards I have been dealt, I'm figuring it out and just like you, I make mistakes. Let's support our fellow moms. Spilled some milk? Don't worry, we've got the mop!

As a reminder, take care of yourself.

With love, Kristina

WANT TO JOIN BOSS MOMS CLUB?

Visit **www.bossmomsclub.com** so you can:

1. Access **Boss Moms Club** wellness retreats and events

2. Subscribe to the **Boss Moms Club** monthly newsletter

3. Join our **Boss Moms Club** community on Facebook

4. Subscribe to our **Boss Moms Club** Youtube page

5. Subscribe to our **Boss Moms Club** podcast

6. Meet other moms like you

Stay connected for future book releases and events.

ACKNOWLEDGEMENTS

To Mariah, Eric Jr. and Da' Jour - My journey as a mother started with you. You have all inspired me in so many ways to never give up on my dreams and to keep pushing forward even when I grow tired. My motivation to become self-reliant and independent derived out of my will to provide the life for you that I never had. I love you all so very much.

Mariah, when I look at you, it's hard not to see myself when I was your age. Thank you for being supportive when you know mommy's had a rough day. Everything I do today is for you tomorrow. You make a habit to remind me about my goals I haven't reached. This guide for moms was my idea, but you pushed me. I hope me publishing this book reminds you that you can do anything you put your mind to. Dedication, persistence and hard work never fail an end result. The choice is always yours. This one is for you baby love. I love you.

To my mother, Cecilia - I know that raising me alone was not easy. Thank you for giving me good genes. From you, I have definitely received my eagerness to prevail against all obstacles, my drive to succeed, and my curiosity to seek answers to every raised question, especially to prove a point that I am right! Lol. We have been through some difficult times together. I watched you go through many struggles yourself as you continued to put food on the table and turn my bedroom light out at night. We didn't always agree, and I know you too were trying to figure it all out. Thank you for never giving up on me. I love you.

To my Nana, Carolyn - You embody so much love and compassion in your heart. I know that your placement in my life was by soul attachment and not by accident. We are so different, but yet so alike. Thank you for always listening to me with no judgment. You are the friend I didn't know I needed. I love you to the moon and back.

To my best friend, Jennifer - Where do I begin? You watched me through all of my struggles as a young teen, a mom and now a grown woman. Thank you for always being there for me and never judging me for my decisions (even though I made some crazy ones lol). Another soul-match made in the heavens, I don't know what I would have done without you in my life. I love you.

RESOURCES

I am a huge believer in personal development.
These books have helped me tremendously in self reflection and growth:

Attached By Amir Levine, Rachel Heller

The Energy Bus By Jon Gordon

The Subtle Art of Not Giving a F*ck By Mark Manson

The One Thing By Gary Keller and Jay Papasan

Rich Dad Poor Dad By Robert Kiyosaki and Sharon Lechter

The Intelligent Investor By Benjamin Graham

Faith: *Transformation Church* w/ Pastor Michael Todd

Boss Moms Club
www.bossmomsclub.com
Boss Moms Club Podcast

All inquiries for speaking events and collaborations should be emailed to support@bossmomsclub.com

Soul Purpose Foundation

To learn more about our giving back initiative or to donate please visit us at: www.soulpurposefoundation.org

BMC GLOSSARY

Un-single: used as an opposite of the term single; a persons relationship status; used when someone no longer wants to be single. **Example:** How does she expect to un-single herself if she doesn't get out of the damn house?!

Sex in the hood: Sex while experiencing motherhood; hood is referenced as a location for motherhood, parenthood or fatherhood; sex in motherhood or sex in parenthood; the sex life of a mother or father; sex while single, married or in a relationship; when a mother or father is dating; when the mother or father is with-holding sex; when parenting gets in the way of having sex or creates a barrier to sexual satisfaction due to time conflicts or other reasons. **Example:** Sex in the hood now a days is rough. I can't seem to find the time to get out; having sex in the hood is hard; I'm just trying to have sex in the hood and everyone is all up in my business.

Mom-Hood: motherhood; parenthood; a mom community; a location; a place where moms often send reminders to friends, family or children of who they are; a mom who is hood with other mothers; **Example:** Theres no place like mom-hood; From my early days of mom-hood, I learned that I have to take time out of the day for myself.

Spilled Milk: used to explain a situation in reference to a mess thats not an object; a situation that appears hard to overcome or causing physical or emotional stress; to minimize the situation so you look at the brighter side and stay focused on your goal; when referencing to the phrase, look at the bigger picture. Example: That was spilled milk, but she cleaned that shit up and went on about her day.

Chores: actions of self care. Example: getting a massage; going to doctor appointments; getting your hair done; going on vacation.

My 10 Step Action Plan

1.

2.

3.

4.

5.

6.

7.

8.

9.

10

ABOUT THE AUTHOR

KRISTINA BUCKNER is a leading expert in motherhood. She is the founder of *Boss Moms Club*, whose mission is to support moms and provide them with an environment where they can be reminded that moms can be women too.

Kristina is also the former producer for a sports and entertainment show *Ballerz World Live*. This show featured NBA news and players on **ESPN** Radio and livestream service in Los Angeles, CA. Kristina brought her talents in organization, direction and vision to help lead in 28 successful shows aired.

An avid community volunteer, Kristina also founded the Soul Purpose Foundation in 2018. This organization focuses on exemplifying the greater good in humanity through its involvement in community efforts that push the needle forward and lend a helping hand to all ages. Kristina has fundraised for several organizations, large and small, including the **Lung Cancer Research Foundation**, where she raised close to $40,000 in donations in her first year. As a runner at heart, Kristina's interest in directing her first 5K came after the loss of her loved one, Gladys, who lost her battle to lung cancer in 2018. Kristina remains dedicated to the cause and offers support wherever she can.

Throughout the course of Kristina's life, she has committed more than 10,000 hours to date towards community service. She has earned and received many awards. In 2024 she received the **Presidential Lifetime Achievement Award** from the White House as well as the Servant Leadership Award from the *Black Chamber of Commerce*.

Dedication is nothing new to this mom. She once drove 3 hours a day, 5 days a week for 2.5 years to complete her Science degree in Dental Hygiene. In addition to her many years in the field of dentistry, Kristina has had a distinguished career in the real estate industry as well, having sold million-dollar homes and even invested in real estate herself. Kristina is also one of the few women of color locally in her field to hold both local and regional positions and has been recognized by major outlets including the **Los Angeles Union Tribune**.

Also known for her appearance on *Let's Make A Deal* with Wayne Brady, Kristina's presence in the entertainment industry has made its mark in history. As an aspiring model, she also starred in music videos with the likes of music artist T.I. and has appeared in movies, local news and sports segments, TV shows, as well as commercials. She was also a digital character in a video game for SONY and has produced, directed, and acted in her own short films.

Kristina, who became a teen mom at the age of 15, achieved significant milestones despite her early responsibilities. At 17, she purchased her first car, and by 20, she leased her own apartment. She credits much of her success to her decision to move to Georgia for college. Upon returning to San Diego, CA, at 26, Kristina was earning a six-figure salary. At 30, she took the bold step of starting her own business and has continued to forge ahead without hesitation.

ADVERTISEMENTS

You can find this coffee mug and more merchandise online at www.bossmomsclub.com